Expressions Of Life, Love, and Wanting

By
Michael Brown

Copyright © 2017
Michael Brown
REVISED EDITION
MAY 2018

Bethune Publishing House, Inc.
The Bethune Group

All rights reserved, including the right to reproduce this work in any form whatsoever without written permission from the publisher, except for brief passages in connection with a review. Photographs may not be reproduced without written permission of the owner.

For information write:
Bethune Publishing House, Inc.
P. O. Box 2008 Daytona Beach, FL 32115-2008
docbethune@tbginc.org

Jacket designed by John-Mark McLeod
J2maginations, LLC
J2maginations@gmail.com

Book design and page layout by
Bethune Publishing House, Inc.
Printed in the United States of America

Library of Congress Control Number: 2017910830
ISBN: 9781945566065

Michael Brown   **Expressions of Life, Love and Wanting**

Poems

POEM	PG
My So Beautiful	6
I See Only You	7
If Only I Had Her	8
Thankful	9
My Everything	10
I'm Missing You	11
My Best Friend	12
Things Change	13
What Am Going to Do for You	14
To My New Love	15
Let Me	16
Red Flag	17
Live Your Life	18
Misery	19
My Man	20
Letter of Passion	21
Captured	23
Angel of Ecstasy	24
Beware	25
Cupids Betrayal	26
Egyptian Flower	27
Male Trait	28
Love Woke Me Up	30
Angry Love	31
Problems	32
Angelic Desires for My Beloved	33
Satisfied	34
To My Other Half	35
Virgin Passion	36

Michael Brown **Expressions of Life, Love and Wanting**

POEM	PG
A Sad Day for Beauty	37
Could Be an Angel	38
You Are	40
You Give Me Life	41
Learn to Let It Go	42
Your Spirit	43
Because I Love Him	44
Dream On	45
The Last Dagger	46
Just Don't Leave Me	47
It Sometimes Happens	48
Love Has No Equal	49
All I Need Is You	50
Chip Off the Ole Block	51
The Creator's Smile	53
Love's Bounty	53
Message to the Men of the World	54
Enslavement	56
Knowledge	56
Knowing Who You Are	57
Love	57

Acknowledgements

Thank you to Marge Clauser for your organizing skills and your patience. I would like to thank Donna M. Gray- Banks for her push. I tend to procrastinate, so thank you Donna for your encouragement. And last but certainly not least, I would like to thank my Grandmother, Mrs. Jesse Mae Coleman Akins, for being a beautiful person and who is now an ancestor. I love you....

Expressions Of Life, Love, and Wanting

My So Beautiful

My so Beautiful, come and go with me to a far-off land and let the grapes of love burst into wine and intoxicate our hearts.

My So Beautiful, come close to me and let my joy make a pilgrimage to solitude and comfort. Let our togetherness have a sweet taste of forever and our souls learn not to weep.

My So Beautiful, let me take you where your deepest explosions have yet to venture, let me nourish your soul as you do mine. I will feed your body ever so sweetly to cause your greatest satisfaction.

The dawn of spring has unfolded and my hunger for your pleasure is anew.

The measure of my love cannot be determined by any calculation or thought. My heart, my body, is yours. You make all of the fibers of my being explode with passion.

Endless affections are exclusively yours which are designed to germinate into your excitement and formulate into a bounteous delight.

You have filled my heart with love. You have become my enchantress and my beautiful swan.

Forever you will be My So Beautiful.

I See Only You

Opium dreams of you fuel my appetite and my desires are to partake of your scrumptious fruits.

My soul has no shame hungering for your flames. Your art of feminine seductiveness and exotic charm lures me into a web of magical rhapsodies.

I float on the perfume of your flesh and have been blessed to bathe in the cool stream of your embrace.

I feel bizarre, unfamiliar emotions that my heart cannot interpret because I have never experienced your kind love, a divine love.

A love that sings a melody of life, an ineffable love, a love that is so righteous that is seems like a sorceress' Spell.

To you I give my all and there is no value owing.

You have the full sum of my heart and there are no affections to be shared with another.

My soul is yours and my eyes see no other.

I see only you.

If Only I Had Her

I lingered in the shyness of self, longing for her

delight. My mind's sight was blurred by her radiance.

Who so sweet as she, what sight her equal.

My speech betrayed me as I longed to sing a
salutation. May I ask your name?

Desires to acquaint myself dominated my
hunger and my courage pushed my intentions.

Oh, how I long for this sweet spice that intoxicates
my senses. The apprehension of my spirit forgot its
agony when a fresh thought entered my mind,
"Maybe she sees me as her jewel?"

What would I say to her to steal her heart?
What would I say to sell myself and win her attention?
If the chance arose I would tell her:

If only I had you I would bathe you in the warm
waters of my heart. I would serenade you with the
colors of a rainbow and caress your every thought
of ecstasy.

I would grant every pleasure that your desires convey.

If only I had you, I would kiss you to sleep
and awaken you with thoughts and spend
endless nights expressing your worth

I hope you would love me, and in return I will
love you forever.

If only I had you.

Thankful

You are my autumn song, my sweet spirit of renewal. No longer does the river of loneliness flow through the valley of emotions in my mind.

Your sweet love hides herself well but the hunger of my heart searches for its delight and when found, I satiate my passion in its majestic vibrations.

The candle of your heart shines on my love and brightens my hopes and desires.

Sorrow no longer drinks up my joy and leaves me empty with yearning.

With you I have an awakening, a newness of my beginning. I cherish you with the sweetness of everything beautiful.

My heart's nourishment comes from your electrifying kisses, your angelic heavenly touch and the soothing tempo of your lovely voice.

You have caused my heart to feel the joys of love once again and I am thankful, thankful for your every breath, thankful for you loving me.

My Everything

A silent whisper flows from your eyes and my heart is lavished with tenderness.

The elements have formed a love that is ours only and There is no other combination that can be our equal.

Your love is heavenly and with one joyous bound I fly to heaven to taste the sweet flavors of your heart.

I have pierced the soul of your delight and await the intimacy that will be bestowed upon us.

Your love is a tender affection that has made you my friend, my lover and my existence.

I'm Missing You

I'm missing you, you're so far away

I'm missing you because a minute seems like a day

I'm missing your beautiful sunshine smile

I'm missing you, because you've been gone for a while

I'm missing your sweet tender touch

I'm missing your laughter that means so much

I'm missing you and running my fingers through your hair

I'm missing your sensual seductive stare

I'm missing you, baby, holding me tight

I'm missing the sweet kisses we share at night

I'm missing snuggling with you while watching tv

Yes, I'm missing you, girl, being close to me

So, can you please come out of the bathroom now

Your ten minutes are up!

I'm just missing you.

My Best Friend

My best friend, she's beautiful and smart and she makes me laugh all the time.

She has always been there for me through thick and thin.

Sometimes we go on trips together and we have the best of times. We go bike riding ang jogging and swimming together.

I just don't do that girly thing with her and that's shopping.

I really don't miss anyone else when we're together no matter where we go.

Whenever she has a problem she knows that she can come to me because we can talk about anything.

I'm with my best friend so much that people say we are starting to look alike.

She's so special to me and it's great to have a best friend like her. I love my wife.

Things Change

I hear the cries of the wind crying a laughing melody of love lost. Crushed dreams echo in loves' den a sadness born of unbearable reality. Love that once soared high now lies on the valley's floor with no chance of recovery.

There's a storm ranging yet there's no feel of rain pouring on my frustration or my confusion.

Oh, how fast the glories of love are lost. How easy hearts of steel can be shattered and fall like glass from ten thousand feet of nowhere.

The depth of my spirit is made shallow when loves' light is made dim. Yesterday the sun was my companion and today the darkness abounds in my heart. When angels betray, is there any hope for true love? When perfection fails, and chaos flourishes can happiness give birth?

There's a monster of loneliness in my heart where joy once dwelled. Kisses are now chased away, embraces are missing, love once alive is now fearful of hurt and will not manifest.

How can one reap the agony and change of caring when one has not sown? No transgressions have I committed for this misery to be upon me. Love is like the wind at times. It changes direction at any time, at any moment.

The reality of life and love is real, and nothing is sure. There's always the possibilities and realities that things change. And when home becomes a stranger, so does love.

What Am I Going to Do for You?

You told me that you'll love me, and we'll live happily and then you asked me, "what are you going to do for me?" So, then I thought for a moment of what I was going to do. Now sit down and listen to what I'm going to do for you:

I'm going to love you 'til the sun refuses to shine
I'm going to love you beyond the span of time.

I'm going to love you like you desire.
I'm going to love you and set your soul on fire

I'm going to make all of your dreams come true
I'm going to let you know there's nothing I won't do for you
I'm going to satisfy your every need
I'm going to encourage you, so you can succeed

I'm going to treat you just like a queen
I'm going to make sure you look good when you step out on the scene. I'm going to make you laugh and smile and bring you joy.
I'm going to make love to you, so you'll know it's the real McCoy

I'm going to make you know what love is all about.
I'm going to make sure with my love you'll have no doubt.
I'm going to show you the spiritual side of me I'm going to love you baby endlessly

I'm going to show you, your love I appreciate
I'm going to show you I'm your life long soul mate
I hope your question was answered, I hope you feel better If you have any doubt again, just re-read this letter
I'm going to love you till the sun refuses to shine.

To My New Love

To my new love – I cherish and celebrate you with a coalition of fruitful interpretations and gratitude.

Riding the new waves of passion there's an opening for love in the air and I have grasped its presence.

Since you came into my life, there's a marvelous love that shines from my filtered eyes and tenderly propels me into the unescapable tentacles of emotions.

I am now lost in sunshine's golden glow and my life is dripping with honey.

You take my breath away and it is you who shines my sky blue.

Old memories just fade away and make way for new illustrious streams of joy and love to flow into our mystic desires.

With you, my search for love is over. I now have that beautiful sunrise and that beautiful sunset, that beautiful moonlit sky.

I have it all with you – my beautiful new love.

Let Me

From within your heart I see the unborn
ecstasies ready to surrender its pleasures on
our love.

The natural law of love is buried in the
bosom of all ages, but the hour of our love
is now.

My desires flourish like a hungry flower
receiving its nourishment from the rain.

Let me enrich your heart with love. Let me
live in your heart to make your heart sing
like a nightingale.

Let me whisper soft enchanting expressions in
your ears, like before the sunset was beautiful,
before the rainbow was radiant the mysteries of
beauty had already adorned your face.

Let me inhale your essence and feel the amazing
beauty of your touch.

You are my mistress of sweetness; my desires have
entered into your house of eternity and I have been
raptured to the height of celebration.

Let me drink the sweet nectar of your bounty because
only with you in my world will my heart be filled.

Red Flag

Around his head was a halo, but it was shaped like a
pretzel instead of round – I didn't see the Red Flag –

His tongue was quick with expression but
without thought – I didn't see the Red Flag –

His gifts were nonexistent, but his taking was constant
- I didn't see the Red Flag –

His smile was twisted but gave just enough
deceiving joy - I didn't see the Red Flag –

His promises never manifested into reality,
phantoms they remained –
I didn't see the Red Flag –

He gave just enough sweet promises that kept me
blind and I slowly regressed –
I didn't see the Red Flag –

The loans and borrowing money I never got back -

I didn't see the Red Flag –

Love and loneliness blurred my senses or maybe -
I didn't want to see –

A hunger and a desire for love and a fear of
being alone almost destroyed me –

Now I've opened my eyes and I've learned to be
alone- I found that strength within –

I've learned to love and depend on myself instead of
depending on men.

Live Your Life

Your high uppity morals keep you dormant and life just passes you by –

You only go around once in this world, so live before you die –

Be safe in your adventures, get out and live a good life –

Don't wait until you get a hundred years old to try one little vice –

All you do is sit at home lonely, or your sitting on the phone yappin' –

You gotta get out in the world and work to make good things happen –

A week now seems just like a day and time is passing you by –

Five, ten years will pass you quickly so go on out and try –

You might even find "Mister Right", who knows, you never know –

Things will never happen for you if you're afraid to go –

Yeah, now I've got you thinking and you're saying, "You know I think I should" –

So, go on out and enjoy your life and make yourself feel good –

If you don't use it – You will lose it.

Misery

Love so strong and love so bold
One mistake causes a shattered soul

Another lost heart, agony and grief;
Loneliness and despair with no relief

Vows taken lightly, promises broken;
Injurious words, not meant but spoken

Confusion lays upon the heart
Pain abounds from being apart.

Rain from your tears will water your strength
Time will heal all and you'll come to your senses

Just remember one thing, love is no game Just
a slip of infidelity can cause much pain

How do I know these things?

Well, you've heard of me
I'm your lovely little friend called "Misery".

My Man

As I looked from afar I saw this magnificent figure heading to an unknown destination. I saw him, but he couldn't see me.

As he walked with authority it seemed the trees and flowers all bowed to his approach.

With broad shoulders and an air of confidence you could see he was sure of himself and the fitting of his clothes reveal his muscular build.

The evidence of my piercing attraction must have caught his attention and he turned my way, our eyes locked and a smile formulated on my face that would have put beauty to shame.

As he came close an appreciation filled my heart. I could see that any woman would love to have a man like that.

What became my greatest joy was that, that beautiful man was my man, out and about, and from afar I saw what I had, and I saw what every woman desired and that was a man like my man.

Letter of Passion

You set the mood for ecstasy with your eyes and I helplessly respond to your every revelation of desire.

Now aroused I ignite the mood for love, my body is now programmed and pulsating with a jumping anticipation of you.

With eager throbs of excitement, I advance my aggression, gently.

Slowly I caress your body, smelling the hypnotic aroma of your paralyzing perfume.

Filled with sonic passion of sensitivity my lips now burn with an unearthly aggression to kiss you.

Tasting the pure honey flavor of your blood ripened lips on mine, I am no more. The engine of my passion is programmed to work for your satisfaction, programmed to ensure your orgasmic explosion is memorable.

Kissing you hungrily, I lay you down on the object of our travel to intimacy, my endeavor is to awaken the deepest fibers of your emotions and activate the most sensitive feelings of sensuality that your body can muster.

My descent upon you is slow and melodic with a gentle hand that touches all – and now I am enjoying every expression of you, every expression.

Eagerly, yet patiently I stimulate the highway
that leads to the object of my wanting.

Your body and your caress expresses "take me, I'm
yours, love me strong and long" and I gladly obey.

As I bid your request we become one as we
share an illustrious harmony in ecstasy and
passion.

Captured

My body smiles, knowing the pleasure it will
encounter in the midst of the day.

Expectation of tenderness causes my
heart to skip a beat.

A child's joy overtakes my adult maturity
and causes me to regress back to my
childhood expressions.

The excitement of your love is
overwhelming, and I am joyously gratified.

Without battle, I surrender my heart to
the on-rush of an entity more powerful
than my resistance.

No, I'm not like the wild animal who wills
to be free. In my desires and my heart, I
secretly desire to be captured, therefore
exposing myself to the hunter's snare.

Now captured by your love I am thrown
into the dungeons of passion and desires
with no desires or strategy of escape.

My happiness is now magnified being
captured and imprisoned by the chains of
your love, and I am joyously captured,
and forever yours.

Angel of Ecstasy

At night when you fall asleep, I enter your bedroom and stand over you. There's a deep feeling of love and affection that causes me to bend down and kiss you ever so tenderly in your unconscious state. Your lips, your, neck, your breast and your thighs all get special attention.

Then slowly I undress you with my imagination and feel the flames of passion that naturally flow from your body. Once again, I caress your succulent breast with the burning desires of my lips and massage your pleasure with mine, slowly penetrating the essence of your body. I feel the tremble of your body with satisfaction and that lets me know that my presence has fulfilled your longings.

As the magical time allotted to me has expired I stubbornly linger, defying the time limit given to me. Hating to give up the night and separating myself from you, I gather my strength and kiss you one more time before I depart.

I hope I have been your satisfier, soothing the craving of desire and arousal. I hope you have enjoyed the beautiful melody of touch, for now I must ascend into the face of the sky and await once again for your inviting and enticing passions to beckon me. Good night my love and may the night have been as wonderful for you as it has for me.

Your Angel of Ecstasy

Beware

When the word "BEWARE" is not heeded and the ears of the heart go silent, the compass and navigation of awareness is lost in the travels of love.

The fog of heartache and betrayal cause the vessel of emotions to become blind and crash in to the rocks of destruction.

When the warning of "BEWARE" is expressed – let wisdom profit.

While basking in the beauty of love – look both ways.

Love, togetherness, faithfulness, trust, and communication are not to be taken for granted. When those virtues are not a part of your awareness, the heart is exposed for banishment and pain.

Cupid's Betrayal

I saw her from afar and desired her to be
mine. I had a well-planned strategy –
to have Cupid shoot his arrow in her heart and
she would fall in love with me.

So, I summoned the master and made my request
and he was willing to bid my command–
Not knowing in his heart lurked betrayal,
of which he could not understand.

He spread his wings and started his journey
to carry out the request for me –
But he was unprepared to behold the beauty
that he was about to see.

Of all the women Cupid had seen, she was
more beautiful than anyone else –
Cupid refused to shoot his arrow in her heart
for me and decided to keep her for himself.

Egyptian Flower

Fashioned from the highest echelon of nature's creativity, your beauty is as rare as a rainbow on the African Plain.

No woman can boast of such beauty.

The savage beauty of Cleopatra is but a tame little kitten when compared to your majestic elegance.

At the time of your creation the flowers in heaven's garden rejoiced and the dawn and the rainbow danced a dance of joy.

Soft as the flow of the Nile, no touch is like caressing your warm silky body, even for an instant.

I laugh at the term goddess to describe your status.

When compared to you a goddess is but a mere servant, a god is but a beggar, and life itself is but a penny on the streets of Thebes.

To gaze into your enchanting eyes is like a honeybee drawn helplessly to the sweet flavor of nectar.

To be kissed by your lips is to be weakened into submission to your every command, and to be possessed by your alluring magic is found with no regret.

Male Trait

My noble heart I must question. My honor and loyalty is being challenged. My eyes that once focused on you only have strayed from the commitment of monogamy and I am perplexed.

My heart has danced only for you, yet I hear a soft whisper of a muffled alluring melody and my body uncontrollably sways to the rhythms that invade my senses.

With you, my love, trust and loyalty are fixed and my warrior's heart I banned from the attraction of another flower. Yet I must check and question this invading feeling. My heart is in disarray and in a dilemma.

My love for you has revealed the culprit, it has exposed the unexplained feeling. The culprit is the animalistic male desires for the unfamiliar. Love has exposed this nature embedded in my sexuality. Male desires that leads one to stray and play have awakened.

The melodic choir of another flower has beckoned my sheep's mentality to follow the path of betrayal. But my love for you is my shepherd and my love leads me back to you.

Though the male trait is powerful, and the nectar of another flower is sometimes tempting, my love and strength will not let the agony and pain of betrayal engage your fragile heart.

I promise, you are safe with your heart in my hands, because remember this, my heart is in your hands.

Also, the female trait is embedded in your nature and I hope that love for me will be your armor when betrayal and desires intrude. Love is always a two-way affair and betrayal will challenge the female heart too.

Love Woke Me Up

At the moment sleep released me this morning, love woke me up and beautiful you were on my mind.

At the moment sleep released me this morning love woke me up, and I saw that I am a mirror of your essence and that reveals to me that I am loved.

Love woke me up this morning and I desire to be whatever you want me to be. I'll be your secret fantasies and adventures, or I'll be still and let your time be your own.

At the moment sleep released me this morning and woke me up, the first thing I saw was your lovely face.

I wish to say I love you, but my tongue labored to interpret that which was in the heart.

At times, my words get suffocated by my inability to find the words to tell you how much I love you.

So, in moments of silence when I'm not talking and just staring at you, know that in that moment of silence I'm expressing what words cannot convey.

At the moment sleep released me and love woke me up, I was awakened from gentle dreams of you and thrust into the reality of joy.

I was awakened to the reality of you. I was awakened to the reality of you loving me when love woke me up.

Angry Love

Ring, Ring. Hello. Hello its Janice. Hey Janice, I'm surprised you called.

I got your letter and was kind of puzzled. It seems you're still angry with me after we split up ten months ago.

Well I am.

I don't think it takes ten pages to express not wanting to be with me. There must be something more than this letter is trying to say.

As angry as you sound it doesn't sound like closure. With all of that anger it sounds like you may still have love for me no matter how angry your letter sounds.

Yeah right.

Listen, I still care for you. If you still have love for me and you still want to be with me even though you said you never want to be with me ever again.

Meet me at our favorite restaurant at 7:30 tonight.

If you meant what you said about not ever wanting to see me again, then don't show up and I'll know that that's the end and we both can have closure and move on with our lives.

7:30. Hey Janice, how you doing?
The moral of the story is a prolong expression of anger is sometimes a sign or expression that there is still love in the heart and you still love that person.

Problems

Things will go wrong –

They sometimes do –

Sometimes you have to call on that inner
spirit that is inside of you –

There will be problems you think you can't overcome –

But tackle each and every problem one by one –

Don't let your problems bring you down –

Meet them head on and turn them around –

Some problems are hard to solve, that I will admit –

But you'll never be victorious if you decide to quit –

When all hope seems lost –

Keep your head on straight –

Only you can solve your problems and control
your fate –

All problems can be solved and all storms subside –

Just rely on that indwelling spirit that you have inside –

Angelic Desires for My Beloved

My sweet beloved, when you looked into my eyes with those magical expressions, you caused me to float right up to heaven as when you do when we intertwine in ecstasy.

The angels in heavens don't even ask me why am I up here, they just say, "You must have looked into the eyes of your beloved," and I said, "That's right, I did."

And after a brief conversation with the angels, I started to float a little bit higher, and I saw creatures more powerful than the angels, and when they saw me up that high they said, "You must have kissed the lips of your beloved," and I said, "That's right I did."

I was so amazed that the heavenly being knew my beloved the way they did.

So, I asked them how did they know, my beloved? They said, "You gazed into her eyes and you kissed her sweet lips and floated up to our realm."

They said, "We have looked into the eyes of your beloved from heaven and we've desired to leave heaven to kiss her lips on earth."

As I descended back down to Earth, I told my beloved my experience. I told her knowing how beautiful she is, I can see how angels and the creatures in heaven would give up heaven for heaven, because it's like being in heaven just being with you.

Satisfied

When our eyes touched, you stole my heart, dreams came true and the world became my joy.

In your world, I live a sweet odyssey, I dream dreams of ecstasy and I am filled with you.

My vision of heaven is right here on earth and my desires for an angel has been fulfilled when I loved you.

Why am I lost in your paradise, why am I so enchanted by your innocence?

My heart can know no other, the splendor of your love has changed my world.

I am overwhelmed with flames of your passion and mesmerized by your true and pure love.

A whirlwind of emotions abounds from my head that I cannot explain, nor shall I try to as long as I am woven into your embrace. With that I am satisfied.

To My Other Half

Our eyes did meet –

Our hearts stood still –

Emotions lacking, now fulfilled –

The lonely nights are of the past –

A love bond made that will always last –

I promise faithfully my love so true –

Every passing day my love is anew –

My love I do give away –

I love you truly, I'll always say –

Sad hearts and eyes my being explore –

And I think of you who I adore –

So, blessed to have an angel of mine –

To love beyond the span of time –

Virgin Passion

When I look into your inner eyes, I see the virgin passion that is waiting to explode into wonderful expressions of love and womanhood.

Let me be the one to feel the newness of your fire and explore the height of your ecstasy that will not slumber.

Time has given birth to your womanhood and your nature has ripened for the harvest.

Your throbbing passion cries out for that which you have never experienced but desire so.

Your excitement and desires are so close that they have merged as lovers.

Let my love merge with yours, let me become one with you.

Let me honor your virtue with the proper signature of companionship, and of love and matrimony so that our entwining will be righteous.

A Sad Day for Beauty

Oh, how beautiful the stars in sky and
how beautiful the sun rise –

Oh, how beautiful the flowers that bloom in
Spring and the clouds in the sky –

Oh, how beautiful a waterfall is and the moon
that glows at night –

My what a beautiful thing to see when a
butterfly takes flight –

Oh, how beautiful are mountains, rivers, valleys
and rolling green hills –

Oh, how beautiful the colorful leaves in Spring
that mystifies and thrills –

Now all these things of beauty are
beautiful, that I'll say is true –

But their beauty seems so dull and pale
when they are compared to you.

Could Be an Angel

Karen was standing on the corner waiting for her next trick to come by. You see Karen was a lady of the night.

One night while she was working the red-light district, she saw this old lady trying to cross the busy street and decided to help her cross to the other side.

The old lady asked Karen, "Baby why is a pretty girl like you out here selling your body when you should be in school?"

Karen said, "I can't seem to find a job and I have a child to feed," Karen helped the old lady to her front door and the old lady said, "I'll pray for you, Baby, to find a job. Now you be safe."

On the way back to the red-light district, Karen felt good about what she did, helping the old lady. Right then she had a change of heart. Something the old lady said touched her heart and she decided to change her life.

On the way home, a John pulled up next to Karen. He got out of his car and tried to persuade her to be with him, but she said I don't do that anymore. Buthe didn't accept that, and he smacked her and forced her into the car. He drove her into the woods and raped her. To keep her from identifying him, he stabbed her with his knife and drove off.

As she laid there bleeding to death she thought, "I know I won't go to heaven because of the life I've lead" and she wondered what will happen to her child.

Slowly her breath left her body and Karen died alone in the woods. When she was found and identified they gave her daughter to her brother to raise.

Karen had no hope and she knew her fate was going to be the opposite of heaven because of the life she lived.

But when Karen's spirit arose she was standing at the pearly gates and she saw this bright light coming towards her. It opened the gate and extended its hand to her.

You see it was that little old lady that she helped home. That old lady was an angel and knew the change of Karen's heart.

When Karen decided to repent and change her life, she showed an act of kindness and her heart won her forgiveness and a place within the pearly gates.

You Are

You are as precious as the rain that falls in spring –

You are a joy to my heart, you're my everything –

You are to me a dream come true –

You are a special love given only to a precious few –

You are like a flower that blossoms in
the middle of the day –

You are a holy love, in a spiritual kind of way –

You are that love I've searched for to make my own –

You are the love that found me and now I'm not alone

You are the love of my life and we'll
always be together –

You are my amazing love that I will love forever –

You Give Me Life

Your sweet love has been my playground and
your lovely smile has been my fortune.

You light up my life and the rays of your beauty shine
waves of happiness on my being.

Is it possible to love you more? Can the melody of
our love be more melodic?

Sometimes I miss you, and you're right here with
me. This love will last forever, and I want the world
to see what you mean to me.

As the rainbow is always beautiful so is your
lovely spirit.
As the taste of honey is always sweet, so are your
kisses.

Your sweet embrace gives birth to me, and
your sacred love makes my heart walk slowly
into your control.

As the rain nourishes the earth, so does your love
nourish my soul and fuel the fire in my heart.

I'm no longer like a drying river or a fading flower.
Your love has rescued me and regenerated my
passions.

With your love, you give me life and with my life I give
you love.

Learn to Let It Go

I once had a mate that I loved, our relationship was tight.

We'd go to movies, dinner and picnics, everything was right.

Then one day we had an argument, it really wasn't that bad.

In fact, it was the first disagreement that we ever had.

She expressed her views, she was done, now all she wanted was peace.

But I was still mad as hell, I was still showing my claws and teeth.

So, she did something to me she really took me to school.

She let me argue by myself and that made me look like a fool.

From that day until now, I learned a lesson that everyone should know.

And that is argue your point any way you want but then learn to let it go.

Your Spirit

Your spirit flows like the white waters of a mighty river. Your sweet presence settles on my heart like the thunderous clouds that settle on top of a mountain revealing a beauty of wonder and excitement.

Your insatiable desires intoxicate me and replenish my strength.

Gazing into your brown sugar eyes has a hypnotic effect that controls me with your simple command.

From you my inheritance is joy, a joy that is undefined and a joy that can never fade away.

Your essence is harmony and grace and that quality that defines you causes salacious emotions to erupt in my soul. These emotions I cannot harness so I let them run free as your spirit.

In time of struggle you have been my compass, in the midst of a storm you have covered me with your wisdom and friendship and I have been blessed by your marvelous spirit that forges me on.

Thank you for being you. The world is so much brighter and beautiful because of your existence and your spirit.

Because I Love Him

He stayed out all night and came home 6:00 this morning with lipstick on his collar. He doesn't show me affection like he used to. I know he's cheating on me. He said it would never happen again. So, I forgave him because I love him.

We went to a party last night and had a nice time until he drank too much, got drunk and smacked me around like he does at home. The next day he said he was sorry, so I let it go because I love home.

The other day I came home from work a little early and caught him in bed with another woman in our home. He said she meant nothing to him. I knew he was sorry because he cried and bought me candy the next day. So, I forgave him because I love him.

I gave my kids a bath last night. I saw they had bruises on their backs. He said he was playing rough with them. I knew it was abuse. I have nowhere to go if I leave so I stay because I love him.

Last night I stood up to him and he gave me a black eye, and then he choked me to death. If only I had the courage and strength to leave, my kids would still have a mother, but I was weak and stayed, because I loved him.

Dream On

Where do dreams go when they don't manifest into reality? Do they wither and fade away like an unwatered rose?

When not accomplished, do dreams fly away to heaven or do they formulate in the imagination of other hopeful hearts.

Dreams are only imagination. In the heart, all dreams prevail with love, all dreams are fulfilled when the heart is true, and the desires are great.

So, dream on, because dreams will come true whether by work or by happenstance.

The Last Dagger

I finally found my rainbow, it was in the tears of my eyes.

I'm sitting here waiting for you to come back to me. My soul is miserable, and I wish I could be back where I belong, in your arms.

My mind is going crazy since you went away. Can one storm change our sweet world?

I ask was our love really love. How can love be broken and end with one disagreement. Your actions have been uncovered.

For when you seek you shall find and what I found was that you never really loved me.

My pain is running deep, but your departure has opened my eyes and has set me free and now my cautions in love have been fortified and I will let this be the last flow of crimson tears that will flow down my face.

Love is not what you say but what you do.

Nothing can be love but love and without love, happiness is an imposter and sex is only a temporary delight!

Without love, dreams will never be tasted and with you I have never tasted its flavors.

So now I make a heartfelt vow, with all of my strength, that your assault on my love will be the last daggers in my heart.

Lesson learned.

Just Don't Leave Me

Leave me but a kiss on my lips and my soul is bound

Leave me but a touch and my spirit soars

Leave me but the words *I love you*, which are profound

Leave me but a peck of passion and I am forever yours

Just don't leave me…

It Sometimes Happens

Hey baby girl, at the coming light, I feel the vibrations of my desires. That early morning love has excited the fullness of my cravings and they are manifested when I feel the master piece of your frame lying next to me. Now I am salivating for the fullness of your womanhood – *Come and get it daddy*…

You see baby, in the moment of this alluring span of time, I not only want you but must have you to quench this turbulent volcano in my body that must be released and that's about to erupt and explode. You understand what I'm saying baby – *Yea baby, I hear you.*

Come close to me baby and take of my bounty that I have to share. Let me hold you close and feel the flesh tones of your body next to mine. Come and get this early morning love and let me love you all morning long – *Ok big daddy*

Come here baby, Oh Yes, there it is, OH YEA baby, all morning long. OH NO! NO! DAMN! DAMN! DAMN!

It's ok big daddy. It sometimes happens. Two minutes is the new *all morning long*. The rooster didn't even crow.

Love Has No Equal

Pleasure can never replace love, love has its own mystique

Passion is never equal with love, even at its highest peak

Ecstasy is an orgasmic explosion, but compared to love it never rises above

No emotion or feeling in the universe can ever equal love

All I Need Is You

For you I have sacrificed wisdom for a blind night in your heart's chambers. I have searched the forest of your divine secrets, longing for the opening of your mysteries.

With the fingers of your passions you have unwrapped the protective powers that surround my heart and now my emotions are laid bare. My heart has folded, and I exchange the freedom of my heart for the desires of laughter.

You have given me your heart and love and If I have caused you in any way to have a joyous heart, that was my intent. If I have cause an awakening in your body that enlightens you of your womanhood, that was my goal.

Your love has taken me to an empyreal plane well beyond the sky, well beyond the consciousness of heaven and now that I am locked in to your ecstasy, my impressions are strong and cannot be impeached.

Let us listen to the song of the rainbow, let us wallow in the passions and desires that have been bestowed upon us. Let's just be us, we, you and me. Let's just let the world go its way. Because in my world…

All I need is you.

Chip Off the Ole Block

Come here son. I don't know why you act the way you do.

Your mother and I act nothing like you and we're your parents.

You see your skin, well that's my skin through genetics.

You see your skin, well that's your mother's skin through genetics.

That blood in your body, well that's my blood through genetics.

That blood in your body, well that's your mother's blood through genetics.

You see this hair on my head, well this is my hair.

You see the hair on your head, well that's your mother's hair not mine.

OOOO Harry, that was a cold, now I see why he acts the way he does.

There is no stronger medicine than love

The Creator's Smile

When God created man, He used his own majestic hands to form man from the dust of the ground.

When God created the animals, He spoke, and they appeared.

But when God created you, He just smiled and there you were.

Love's Bounty

Your love has exposed its bounty to my hungry heart, and I now feast as a starving obese addict, overdosing on your passion.

Message to the Men of the World

This is a message to all of the men all over the world about our women all over the world –

Black, White, Brown, Red and Yellow.

The mysteries of heaven are in her. Life emanates from her womb and she is to be appreciated and adored.
Yet our patriarchal mindset has suppressed her light and arrested her spirit.

The ancestral principle of a masculine and a feminine harmony is the natural harmony of life, but it seems we as men have diminished her from the equation.

We must have her equally by our side and know her value or we will not survive.

We must realize that there is no religion higher than loving and respecting our women.

I ask you, man to man, brother to brother – let's recognize her and honor her and fiercely protect her.

I call for the philosophy of the original mind of man to step forward and restore the Masculine and the Feminine harmony back to a place of balance, so our children can taste the world as it should be and our young men can learn of her value and inner beauty.

To all of the men of the world – honor her for she is the mother of all, she is the origin of life and spirit.

We must let them know their worth, which is everything.

We must care for her like the fragile flower she is and love her in a thousand different ways.

Honor her and you honor your masculinity. We must recognize her matriarchal position in life as she deserves the highest praise.

If we fail to, we as men in the world will not prosper and we will not truly be whole.

Her strength and wisdom make us strong. Her cool and calm nature settles our aggressive nature. Without that humanity falls and the quality of life is diminished.

Only we can sabotage our destiny by neglecting her womanhood. So, love her, respect her, protect her – Because without her we are nothing but a lost spirit devoid of love.

Without her we take away fifty percent of our ability to live and to know thyself. So, for the sake of love – love her.

Enslavement

Too many people have a bitter battle with truth and knowledge and an easy-going relationship with belief and feeling good, and that keeps them in spiritual enslavement. With knowledge, you don't need belief.

Knowledge

In life "pretty" can take you a long way but "smart" can take you all the way.

The surety of knowledge is a love song That lasts forever and inspires your life.

It gives you strength and guides your path to comfort.

Knowing Who You Are

Being conscious of one's self nurtures and indwelling spirituality and gives an awareness to know our selves and with that knowledge of self the path traveled in life is made clear.

Love…

"I leave you love. I leave you hope. I leave you the challenge of developing confidence in one another. I leave you a thirst for education. I leave you a respect for the use of power. I leave you faith. I leave you racial dignity. I leave you a desire to live harmoniously with your fellow men. I leave you finally, a responsibility to our young people."

                        Dr. Mary McLeod Bethune

What's Love got to do with it...?

Everything!

www.ingramcontent.com/pod-product-compliance
Lightning Source LLC
Chambersburg PA
CBHW071544080526

44588CB00011B/1789